Dear Parents,

Children's earliest experiences with stories and books usually involve grown-ups reading to them. However, reading should be active, and as adults, we can help young readers make meaning of the text by prompting them to relate the book to what they already know and to their personal experiences. Our questions will lead them to move beyond the simple story and pictures and encourage them to think beneath the surface. For example, after reading a story about the sleep habits of animals, you might ask, "Do you remember when you moved into a big bed? Could you see the moon out of your window?"

Illustrations in these books are wonderful and can be used in a variety of ways. Your questions about them can direct the child to details and encourage him or her to think about what those details tell us about the story. You might ask the child to find three different "beds" used by animals and insects in the book. Illustrations can even be used to inspire readers to draw their own pictures related to the text.

At the end of each book, there are some suggested questions and activities related to the story. These questions range in difficulty and will help you move young readers from the text itself to thinking skills such as comparing and contrasting, predicting, applying what they learned to new situations and identifying things they want to find out more about. This conversation about their reading may even result in the children becoming the storytellers, rather than simply the listeners!

Harriet Ziefert, M.A.
Language Arts/Reading Specialist

More to Think About

Does a Woodpecker Use a Hammer?

Does a Bear Wear Boots?

Does a Camel Cook Spaghetti?

Does a Panda Go to School?

Does an Owl Wear Eyeglasses?

Does a Tiger Go to the Dentist?

Doe a Hippo Go to the Doctor?

Does a Seal Smile?

Think About where everyone sleeps

Does a Beaver Sleep in a Bed?

Harriet Ziefert • illustrations by **Emily Bolam**

BLUE APPLE

For Sylvie

Text copyright © 2006, 2014 by Harriet Ziefert
Illustrations copyright © 2006 by Emily Bolam
CIP data is available.
Published in the United States 2014 by
🍎 Blue Apple Books
515 Valley Street, Maplewood, NJ 07040
www.blueapplebooks.com
Printed in China
ISBN: 978-1-60905-423-6
1 3 5 7 9 10 8 6 4 2
02/14

Does a baboon sleep in a bed?

No way!
A baboon does not sleep
in a bed.

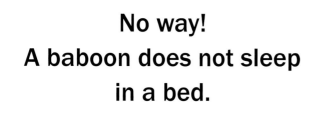

A baboon sleeps in a tree—
usually a different one every night.

Does a beaver sleep in a bed?

A beaver sleeps on a platform inside its lodge.
The platform is above the water.
The entrance is underwater so that enemies,
such as foxes, cannot get in.

Does a polar bear sleep in a bed?

What a silly idea!
A polar bear does not sleep in a bed.

A polar bear sleeps
on the snowy ground
inside a den.

Does a bumblebee sleep in a bed?

Not exactly!
Bees sleep in different places.

This bee is sleeping in a flower.
When the sun comes up
in the morning, it will fly away.

This bee is sleeping
on a bed of wax
in a hole in a tree.

This bee is sleeping
on a bed of gray "paper"
in a hive.

Does a horse sleep in a bed?

No.
A horse sleeps standing up.
It doesn't need a bed.

Does a dog sleep in a bed?

Some dogs do sleep in beds.

Many people have special doggie beds
for their dogs.

But dogs cannot build their own beds.

All animals sleep, but only people sleep
in different kinds of beds.

Some tiny babies
sleep in baskets.

Some sleep on
papoose boards.

Bigger babies and toddlers sleep in cribs.

When a child is old enough,
then it's time for a grown-up bed.

Children sleep in all kinds of beds.

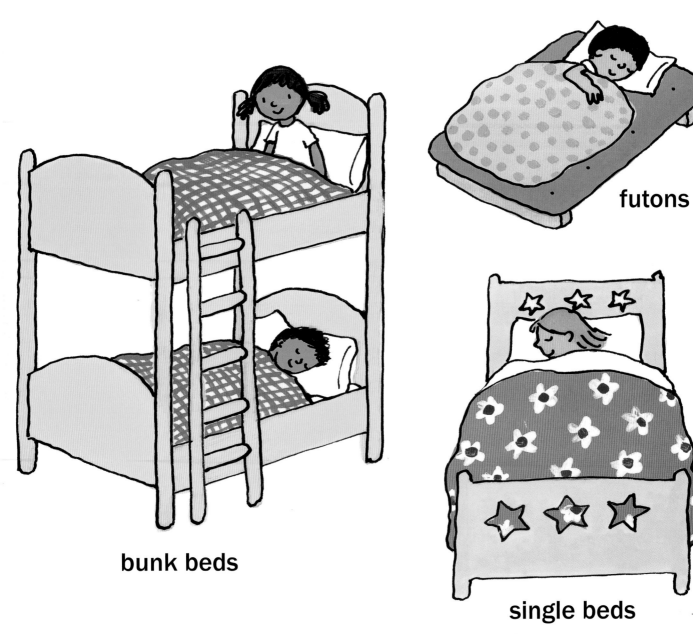

futons

bunk beds

single beds

So do grown-ups.

double beds

hammocks

sleeping bags

People have
high beds...

low beds...

soft beds...

hard beds...

little beds...

and big beds.

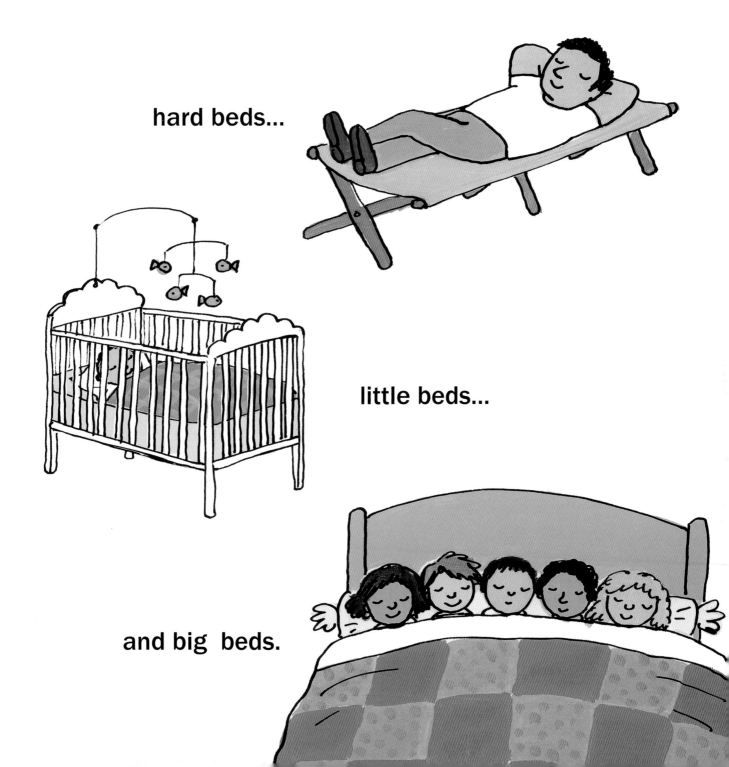

What kind of bed do you sleep in?

Think 💡 About where everyone sleeps

This book compares the sleeping places of a baboon, a beaver, a polar bear, a bumblebee, a horse, and a dog with the places where people sleep.

Compare and Contrast

Watch a pet that you own or someone else owns.

• Where does it sleep? Could you sleep that way?

Ask your family about all the beds you have slept in since you were born.

• Draw the bed you sleep in now.

Sometimes people sleep outdoors.

• Have you ever been camping or slept outdoors?

• How was it different from sleeping in your bed?

• What did you need to fall asleep?

Research

Visit the Animals Section of your library.

• Pull out some interesting books.

• What can you find about how and where animals sleep?
  Make a list.

The beaver makes the door to his house underwater to keep foxes out.

• What other ways do animals stay safe from other animals when they sleep?
  (bird, mouse, panda bear, baboon)

Observe

Watch someone in your family, or a pet, sleeping.

- Do they make sounds, move, or breathe in a way
  that is different than when they are awake?

- Make a list of what you observe.

When you visit a friend's house, ask to see his or her bedroom.

- How is this room different from your room? Draw both rooms.

Write, Tell, or Draw

Does everyone dream?

- Do dogs dream? How could you find out?

- Do you dream? Write a story, or draw a picture, about a dream you had.

**What would it be like to share your bed with one of the animals in this book?
Write or tell about it.**

- Draw yourself in your bed with that animal.